Why God Created Dads

By
Paul E. Sheppard

PRESS

Dedication

This book is dedicated to:

The memory of my father,
the late Dr. Horace W. Sheppard Sr.
My mother, Peggy Sheppard
My wife, Meredith
My two adult children, Alicia and Aaron

Acknowledgments

*M*any thanks to my collaborator, Rob Suggs. I'm also grateful to various bishops, pastors, Christian leaders, and fellow believers who encouraged and supported Meredith and me during my season of restoration. Unfortunately, there are far too many to mention. But please know how much I love and appreciate each of you! However, there are several of you I must acknowledge by name:

Destiny Christian Fellowship
(truly the world's greatest church!)
Pastor John K. Jenkins Sr.
Bishop Timothy J. Clarke
Dr. Richard Allen Farmer
Bishop David Michael Copeland
Pastor Claudette Anderson Copeland
Bishop T. D. Jakes
Bishop M. Tyrone Cushman
Pastor Dick Bernal
Pastor Gerald Simpkins
Ron Walters
My siblings: Pastor H.W. Sheppard Jr., Pat, Gwen, Kenny, and their spouses

Table Of Contents

Chapter 1

"Pop" Culture

*O*n the subject of fathering, there are two important texts.

One is the Bible.

The other is the father who raised us (or did not).

The first is the perfect, unfailing Word of God. The second depends totally upon your experience.

Either way, whether we have a great dad or a deeply flawed or absent one, we know that our fathers leave a vast imprint on our lives. Right or wrong, we tend to learn from them what manhood is. And more importantly, we're prone to see the "heavenly Father" as a super-sized, all powerful version of who our earthly dads are.

I was blessed to have a dad who taught me valuable lessons by both precept and example.

His name is Horace W. Sheppard Sr. I called him Pop.

He went home to be with the Lord on February 22, 2008. I'm grateful for the fact that I didn't have to lose him to love him. I already had a good under-standing of what he had done in my life, and he knew how much I loved him.

I paid my tributes while I could, but it's never enough. I want to honor him again, one more time, in these first two chapters of a book about fathering, because I want to share some of what I learned from his strengths, weaknesses, successes, failures, and undeniable love for God.

I was raised by parents who walked with God, and they raised us so that we would do the same. They brought us up in the training and instruction of the Lord, and they were unapologetic about that.

They were people who looked into the future as they walked through the present. They knew that the best work of their life was to prepare their children to live as followers of Christ. They had no confusion on that assignment; they took it seriously and attended to it every day. And this is a primary reason why my siblings and I all came to know the God they served.

It wasn't just about making certain we received a good education, though they did that. It didn't simply mean teaching us to be kind to others, though they took care of that, too. Everything they taught us was built on the foundation that the fear of the Lord was the beginning of wisdom. They knew that if we could grasp that particular truth, then all things were possible for us; if we didn't, we would miss the most important mark of all.

I'm deeply grateful my parents took so many pains to teach us. And I have grave concerns about this talk I keep hearing: parents questioning whether to talk to their children about God.

"We want our kids to work it out for themselves," they say. "It's not for us to impose anything on them. Their religion is their business."

I have to admit that philosophy is inexplicable to me. I came up in a world without spiritual neutrality—you stand for Jesus, or you're falling for something else. Children don't learn in neutral terms. If you never talk about something, what they gather is that it's not very important to you. And it's highly unlikely to be important to them, because very early in life, children tend to take on our values. Later, they'll be very conscious of forming their own, but by that time their characters will already have foundations based largely on what they saw in us.

Are you neutral about whether they look both ways before crossing the street? Whether they go to grammar school or not? If you take a stand about those things, why not take one about the most important issue of all—who Jesus is?

No Neutral Ground

My parents knew they couldn't get our names on the heavenly rolls. They couldn't force Christ on us. But they could teach us what they knew and demonstrate the power of their convictions. They taught us and loved us right into the kingdom, from the first day we were on this planet. They were intentional about building a Christian family.

Their policy was this: "We can't make you become Christians, but we can make it very hard for you to practice a lifestyle of sin while living in this house! You're only going to be saved when the Lord convicts your heart, and you personally commit your life to Him. But in the meantime, you need to know that this is a household of faith. There will be things off-limits to you simply by virtue of your last name and your street address."

They were right up front with us. They told us how it would be, then they carried it out. They trained us, they loved us, and they nurtured us in the things of God. Their legacy is five adult children who, though imperfect and totally dependent upon the grace of God, love the Lord with our whole hearts.

I have deep admiration and respect for my mother, but the subject of this book is fatherhood. So here in the first section, I want to focus on Pop, and the culture he created.

Pop died at the age of eighty-one. The irony of that was that, for the last forty of those years, he had always thought his final day on earth was just around the corner. He was not one of those people who avoided talking about death; it was a popular subject with him. He brought it up all the time, always convinced that the time of his departure was at hand.

In his forties he liked to say, "I don't believe I'll live to see fifty." We couldn't think of any reason a young man would be talking that way. Frankly, it seemed morbid. He was healthy, he had no life-threatening habits, and his future seemed bright.

But that milestone of fifty was one he was certain he would never reach. When that day came, the church threw him a big birthday party. He laughed, enjoyed the fellowship, and endured teasing from those who were glad his prediction didn't come to pass. I also think he was a little disappointed! That was just Pop.

Another decade came and went, then another; each one against all odds, as far as he was concerned. Then, after forty-five years in pastoral ministry, he retired. The years had finally caught up with him; he had too many physical challenges. He hated retiring, especially because it meant he'd have to miss out on his cherished ambition of dying in the pulpit. "I'd like to preach my best sermon one day," he would say, "then sit down and die—just go home to be with the Lord at the end of a worship service."

We shook our heads and chuckled, but that's how he imagined going out: reach the very summit of your preaching abilities, then just keep on going up into heaven!

Strangely enough, it happened to a friend of his. Another preacher in Philadelphia, on Easter of all Sundays, halted his message mid-sermon and said, "I can't go on." He staggered back to his seat and gave up the ghost. My dad heard about that and was actually jealous! That was *his* idea, and Bishop Jones had stolen it!

Though fixated on dying, he experienced some blessings that come with advanced years. He saw all his children grow up, accept the Lord, and build their own households of faith. He also enjoyed knowing his grandchildren, and even some great-grandchildren.

Famous Last Words

Among his last words, on February 22, 2008, were these: "I'm not going to make it through the day."

At that point, of course, it was like the boy who cried wolf several thousand times. Mom's first thought was, "There he goes again." But there was something a little bit different in his tone—something that told her he might mean it this time.

Later in the day, Pop was in bed and struggling to breathe. Mom was there, along with my sister Gwen. They began rubbing Pop down with ointment to help his airways.

As they did, my dad began to speak, in the manner of an old man who knows he has finally reached his destination, who is already standing in the open doorway to Paradise. "Make sure you tell everyone you took really good care of me. And forgive me for not being a better husband."

That last part had become a constant theme with him. For his entire pastoral career, he had been married to his ministry. Consequently, his wife and children had always known we'd never have the very best of his time and energy. We didn't even know for sure what time he'd be home for dinner! So we learned to eat without him and be content.

After all, he had a bigger family with bigger needs, and that was the congregation God called him to shepherd. We chose not to resent it, because we understood his heart and we knew that his passion for ministry didn't diminish his love for us. But in his final years, he sometimes reflected on his history of misplaced priorities, and acknowledged his need of forgiveness.

"Now I want you to cry," he added as he spoke to Mom.

You may think that's strange, but you had to know my dad. Even on his deathbed, he was soaking in the drama. He liked crying. It's just who he was, the consummate, dramatic people person who had married his natural opposite.

My mother is reserved, quiet, and when she does speak, people listen. Her words are few and crucial. She has never worn her feelings on her sleeve. You have to really know her to be able to tell if she's happy.

I can remember times when we'd have a picnic in the yard. She would pull up a chair, keep an eye on her children, and life was good; she'd be in her element. But you wouldn't know that unless you knew her well. People might ask us, "Is your mom okay?" And we'd have to smile and assure them she couldn't be happier.

Yet Pop wore his emotions on a big neon sign. He could cry at a grocery store opening! When he was growing up, he and a cousin would go to funerals of people they didn't even know, and practice recreational grieving!

One time while in Ohio to conduct a revival, the host pastor was going to officiate a daytime funeral. My father asked him, "Is this going to be a good funeral?"

"How do you define a good funeral?"

"Well, will there be a lot of crying and stuff?"

"I think so."

"Okay then. I'll go with you!"

And sure enough, the pastor looked up at one point and saw Pop crying just as if he'd lost a good friend!

Now, finally preparing to experience death himself, he told my mother, "I want you to cry."

My mother and sister called 911 and asked for emergency medical technicians to be dispatched. Pop stopped dying long enough to say to my sister, "I like that song you're singing. Don't stop singing it."

She was not singing; nonetheless Pop was hearing music. I'm convinced that the angels were tuning up.

As he listened, he closed his eyes in contentment, and they never opened again. Not on this side of the doorway. He was no longer in the waiting room. His number had been called and his divine appointment had come.

According to Luke chapter 19, Zacchaeus had a divine appointment, too. Not one that ended his life on earth, but one that changed it forever. In the next chapter, we'll explore that story—with a little more about Pop.

Chapter 2

Created to be Persistent

*D*o you remember the story of Zacchaeus? He was a chief tax collector, a despised man who climbed a tree in order to catch a glimpse of Jesus as he passed. And then God did something remarkable.

In speaking at Pop's funeral, I compared him to Zacchaeus. The first parallel I mentioned was superficial: both were "height challenged." Zacchaeus is perhaps the most famous "little" man in the Bible, a fellow who had to climb a tree to see over the crowd. As a kid in Sunday School, I was always struck by the flannel board picture of a short man in a "bathrobe" (that's what it looked like to me) climbing a tree.

His was a touching story. Nobody liked Zacchaeus. He knew no one was going to stand aside and let him peek through the forest of elbows and shoulders.

Yet he was determined to see Jesus. So he sacrificed his dignity, shimmied up a sycamore tree, and got a bird's eye view of the man he had heard so much about. And his determination was rewarded as Jesus looked up and saw him too.

My father stood five-feet-four. I'll never forget the time when I was about twelve years old and got one of those adolescent growth spurts going. I shot right past him in height. That's a big moment for a young man, becoming taller than his dad.

But as time went on, I saw clearly that Pop was tall in those ways that really matter. Not all heights are measured in feet and inches.

The most significant comparison between Zacchaeus and my dad is that they both really wanted to see Jesus. Both of them were willing to go out on a limb to get a better view of him. And both of them had their lives changed forever as a result.

Luke 19 tells the story of an ordinary day for Jesus. Jesus was just passing through town, but not by any coincidence. He seems to have gone out of his way to make Jericho a stop, because His heavenly Father had something for him to do there; someone to meet.

That someone was a man with a lot of personal issues. Zacchaeus might as well have walked through town with a sign around his neck marked, "Sinner." That's how people identified him. So it's no wonder that on this day they said, "Look, Jesus is going home with a sinner!" And they were absolutely correct.

Zacchaeus collaborated with the Romans to clean out his own people financially, finding out when they had any money, and then seizing a heaping share of it. By arrangement, the tax collector could keep a very comfortable percentage of his haul; the rest he turned into the Romans.

Often in the gospels we see the phrase, "tax collectors and sinners." In other words, there was all-purpose sin, and then there was tax collecting. It was a despised category unto itself. Even sinners knew tax collectors were sinners!

So Zacchaeus was the kind of man that no one wanted to be seen with. And yet Jesus gladly invited himself into this man's home and into his life.

Another important similarity: God specially targeted Zacchaeus. He targeted my dad also. In eternity past, Pop was a marked man. And that deal was sealed through the prayers of the godly woman who gave birth to him.

My paternal grandmother died at the age of one hundred. She raised ten children despite lacking support from her irresponsible and largely absentee husband. My granddad was a rolling stone, so to speak. He knew how to make babies, but didn't have the character necessary to raise them. Nevertheless, my grandmother leaned on the everlasting arm of God and created a nurturing environment for her children.

"When I was pregnant with your father," she once told me, "I put my hands on my belly and I said, 'Now, Lord, about this one: I want you to make a preacher out of him.'"

So Pop never really had a say in the matter. From the moment he checked into this world, he was a marked man. God and my grandmother had come to an agreement on it.

By the time he had gotten into his teens, however, he looked a lot more like a comedian than a shepherd. There was a man named Eddie "Rochester" Anderson who was a wildly popular comedian on the radio and in movies. He worked with Jack Benny and regularly stole the show. Pop thought he could do that—only better.

He told my grandmother he was on his way to Hollywood, where he would become rich and famous and buy her a big house. He wanted her to know he was going to take good care of her.

My grandmother was disgusted by her son's silver screen ambitions. She said, "Boy, I went to death's door to bring you into this world." She told him about laying her hands on her belly, about talking to God. "I didn't ask God to make you Eddie Rochester," she said. "I asked him to make you *a preacher*. And if you think I'm letting you go to hell by way of Hollywood, you'd better think again. Before that happens, I'll ask God to save you one day and kill you the next!"

That's what I call taking out a prayer contract on your kid! But it shows she believed what the Scriptures teach—that the prayers of the righteous are powerful and effective.

Caught Short

Pop was a teenager, and he was in church one day when there was an altar call. One of the mothers in the church fixed my father dead in her sights and said, "The Lord has somebody here today who needs to get saved."

She felt so certain about my father that she walked down into the congregation, came up to him and said, "God says today is the day of your salvation." Then she took him by the arm and walked him down to the altar.

I asked Pop what that was like, being kind of shanghaied to salvation. "I didn't go under coercion," he said, "because God was talking to me. He was saying, 'This is your day.' And it came into my mind that if I didn't come to God on this day, I might not have a second chance."

Zacchaeus' name meant *righteous* or *pure*, so I have to believe his parents had spiritual hopes for him. Perhaps they had even prayed for him to have a close encounter with God. If so, God answered prayer by setting up divine appointments.

Bartimaeus was a blind beggar in Jericho—and it wasn't such a big town. So it's not a stretch at all to speculate that Zacchaeus, who rubbed shoulders with a lot of people, heard his story and had his curiosity piqued.

And maybe there were others also who had crossed paths with Jesus and bore witness to a miracle. We don't know exactly who God used to whet Zacchaeus' appetite for a new life, but God's purpose was accomplished as this tax collector ran ahead of the crowd and climbed a tree, risking ridicule and possible injury just to catch a glimpse of Jesus.

As a short man, my dad once wondered if he was missing out on some finer things in life. But that question was settled one day when he talked with

Hugh Myers, a deacon in our church.

"Do you ever get tired of being short, like I do?" Pop asked him. "Ever wish you were six feet tall?"

Deacon Myers thought about it for a quick moment and said, "Pastor, let me ask you a few questions. You've got a good wife, right?"

"Sure."

"You have five children you're proud of, right?"

"Yep."

"Spacious house?"

"Of course."

"You make a good living? Drive a nice car? Have a fulfilling job? Good friends?"

"Well, yes, but . . ."

Deacon Myers said, "Just like the tall folks, huh? The only thing they have on you or me is a few inches! They can't do much in life that you or I can't also do—nothing that really counts, anyway."

From that day on, Pop accepted his stature. As a matter of fact, he decided to make it a point of pride. He would say, "I'm a small piece of leather, but I'm well put together."

Zacchaeus was a small piece of leather, too. And the day Jesus was passing through town was a defining moment for him. So he determined that a wall of taller people would not prohibit him from seeing Jesus.

In preparation for this defining moment, God had planted a sycamore tree near the spot where Zacchaeus would stand that day. This was a kind of fig tree with mediocre fruit, but it did have low, spreading branches that were perfect for climbing or for shade. Zacchaeus saw those limbs and had a thought. The next thing he knew, he was perched above everyone else.

When you're caught short, you have to find another way to stand tall. My father had been caught short in factors other than height. For one thing, he had no one to show him what a father should truly be, since his dad was only home for brief intervals.

Pop was caught short in the area of education, never graduating from high school. As a teenager, he had to drop out of school to go to work on the railroads of south Philadelphia and earn money to take care of the family, since his father wasn't around as a breadwinner.

He believed that if he took care of his mother, then God would bless him. And sure enough, that happened. Without the benefit of attending seminary or Bible college, he studied diligently and preached with extraordinary power. In the prime of his career, he was considered by many to be one of the most outstanding Black preachers in America.

One of Pop's legacies is stretched across the USA and even beyond. It is in the hundreds of pastors and leaders he discipled, mentored, and inspired. It's also in the multiplied thousands of men, women, boys, and girls he led to Christ throughout the years.

Loving and Trusting

My father was short in height, short on education, short on role models, but tall on initiative. He ran ahead, climbed above, and rose to overcome his limitations. And among his strongest gifts was the ability to connect with people.

He had a natural love for people, and he understood that poverty had nothing to do with living a quality life. He got around, engaged strangers, made them feel good, converted them into friends, and left them with the knowledge that he cared deeply about them. I used to meet folks whose names Pop had long since forgotten, but they loved him dearly and were sure they were among his closest friends. In terms of loving and being loved, he was a wealthy man indeed.

Yet for many years Pop struggled with a poverty mentality, no doubt derived from his upbringing. So whenever his church wanted to bless him in special ways, he felt guilty accepting it. We'd have to explain, "Pop, God wants to bless you; the people want to bless you. Accepting their generosity gives them a blessing in return."

As he grew older, he learned to loosen up a little bit and let people honor him. On one of his milestone pastoral anniversaries, the church purchased for him his dream car, a Mercedes Benz. To be given such a wonderful gift, when he had grown up poor and dropped out of school, seemed a miracle to him. He would drive that car around, praising God and singing and finding new friends to share his joy.

One day in the early 1990's, I returned to Philly for a visit after having moved to California. I arrived at my parents' home and noticed his Mercedes wasn't in the garage. "Mom," I asked, "where's Dad's car?"

She looked up at me. "They didn't tell you?"

"Tell me what?"

"Well, he was driving around, doing his thing, you know how your father is. He met this man who started talking about the hard times he'd been through. So your dad said, 'Tell you what. I'll pay you to drive me around today while we talk some more.'"

After a few errands, your dad said, 'Drive me to my house. I've got to run in and pick up something.'"

As I heard this, I began to groan. I knew where the story was going. I'll bet you do, too.

Being the loving and trusting man that he was, Pop jumped out of the car and hurried into the house to get whatever he needed. When he came back outside, the car was nowhere to be seen.

Later he discovered that the thief had taken a joyride around Philadelphia that only ended when he crashed into another vehicle; at which time he jumped out, and ran away.

But Pop gladly paid the price of a damaged car as well as many other losses, betrayals, and disappointments in order to keep on connecting with people.

And when it came to money and material things, he was generous to a fault. Over the years, many friends and colleagues tried to convince him of the need to be diligent about saving money and leaving a financial inheritance for his children's children. But what mattered most to Pop was that he'd leave behind a legacy of love for God and others.

Out of Your Tree

After his divine encounter, Zacchaeus opened his heart wide and learned that life isn't about money or the things it can buy. He said in effect, "All that people are saying about me is true, and more. But I'll tell you this. I'm going to make it right. From this day on, I'll give half of all that I have to the poor, and for all you folks I've cheated in the past: I'll repay you four times over."

And that's what Jesus cares about—not what you've done, but what you're going to do next. If you'll make the next decision the right decision, your life can completely change for the better.

Christ changed my dad's life while he was still a teenager, and he spent the rest of his days helping others to experience that same life-changing love.

Then, on February 22, 2008, a shadow fell over Pop as he lay in bed. Jesus was standing there, smiling at him.

I'm sure Pop said, "Lord, is this the day I've been waiting for?"

And Jesus said, "Yes, you're finally going home."

And Pop smiled and closed his eyes, and began to hear that music. At first, he thought my sister was singing. But as he concentrated, he knew there was no music on earth like the melodies and choruses he was hearing.

And within minutes, he opened his eyes in Paradise. And perhaps among those who greeted him was his own father, who accepted Christ very late in life.

Chapter 3

Created to be Purposeful

*I*saiah, the Old Testament prophet, talks about a terrible day when people will have turned away from God. He says it will be characterized by a scarcity of men. "In that day seven women will take hold of one man . . . Take away our disgrace!"(Isaiah 4:1). Interestingly, more than a few churches today are reporting that very ratio of seven to one among their membership.

While Isaiah talks about why the Day of the Lord should be feared, another prophet foretells the hope it will contain.

Malachi wrote the last book in the Old Testament. And listen to what God says through him:

> *"Behold, I will send you Elijah the prophet Before the coming of the great and dreadful day of the LORD. And he will turn The hearts of the fathers to the children, And the hearts*

*of the children to their fathers, Lest
I come and strike the earth with a
curse." Malachi 4:5–6, NKJV*

What does Malachi mean?

He speaks of John the Baptist, who will come in the New Testament and who is closely associated with Elijah. So the Old Testament ends with a promise of a new Elijah, and the gospels introduce us to John the Baptist, the new "Elijah."

But notice what Malachi is saying he will do. *He will turn the hearts of the fathers to the children.* This would be a sign of his ministry.

When revival comes, there is always a softening of men's hearts. There is always an army of men rising up to be what God wants them to be. And their hearts turn to their children and their families. You can set your spiritual watch by this principle. When the Spirit moves, men take a stand for God.

I believe we're living in a time when God's Spirit is calling out for men to come forward, to get their hearts right, to love their families and their churches. God is looking for a few good men. And in society as a whole, if you look to our worst problem spots, if you look toward children who are rebelling and getting on the wrong side of the law, you're also going to find a trail of men who have been derelict in their duty.

Our communities need the men. Our cities and our families and our churches need them. I believe the world would be a very different place if we had a revival of men—in particular, of fathers.

Dads Have Purposes

Thank God for mothers, who seem to hold the world together. They are irreplaceable and almost indestructible. It seems to me that as the men fall by the wayside, the women are always there, taking a double load, a triple load, raising their children and caring for the family's needs. Mothers today are champions.

Having said that, with all the heroism of the women, we must have the men. There's nothing like a man in his place. When men and women serve together, as they are meant to serve, then miracles can happen in this world. We need men to be husbands and fathers—by the Book.

You might well ask, why does it matter? In the twenty-first century, do we really want to make a big deal about men and women? Does it matter which gender does a particular job?

The world says no, but the Bible tells it differently. The Scriptures teach that God created us male and female, and that He does nothing without purpose. He created us with complementary gifts, to be a team; to function as one; to be greater than the sum of the two parts. He created us to come together and bring a family into this world, and tend that family together. Family works best when Mom and Dad work together.

Many people have all but decided the world is rolling downhill too fast to stop. It's an avalanche, they say. The men have slacked off and we're all doomed.

I'm not one of those people. I realize we have problems; what's new about that? I also know that, throughout human history, God has always raised up individuals to bring revival, to turn things around. There is no avalanche strong enough that God can't put the brakes on it.

God is getting His team together. He's looking for men whose hearts are fully committed to Him. And if you haven't been the greatest father, if your kids are already adults, He's still looking at you. You can be a great father of an adult child. You can be a attentive grandfather. You can be a mentor for other fathers or young people.

The foundation God lays for fatherhood can be seen in Matthew 22:37, known as the Great Commandment. In fact, it's a foundation for all of us, not just fathers.

The occasion was one of those question-and-answer sessions the Pharisees loved so much when Jesus was on tour. He wasn't given to press conferences, but they followed Him around like a pack of reporters with their "gotcha" questions. Every now and then, they felt like they had a great one, a true stumper. Once He committed Himself to an answer, they could twist it around to make Him look bad. In other words, they were masters of the loaded question.

In this case, they asked Him, "What is the greatest commandment in the Law?" The idea was to make Him name one law so they could accuse Him of being weaker on the others.

Jesus answered it this way:

"Love the Lord your God with all your heart and with all your soul and with all your mind." This is the first and greatest commandment. And the second is like it: "Love your neighbor as yourself." The Law and the Prophets hang on these two commandments. Matthew 22:37-40

Of course, His answer not only trumped the trick question, but it laid down a deep and foundational teaching about God's priorities—what should be *our* priorities. Jesus was observing that the first four commandments can be boiled down to loving God fully; the last six can be boiled down to loving others appropriately.

Jesus actually reached into Deuteronomy 6:5 to pull out that incredible teaching. It's so comprehensive that you can hang your life on it. Whenever you come to any kind of a decision, you ask, how will this reflect my love for God? How will this reflect my love for people? It's life in a nutshell.

And so we must start there when we talk about fathers: Dad, love God with everything in you. Set your heart on Him.

And by the way—it's a commandment, not a suggestion, not an option, not an exercise to earn bonus points. This is for all of us.

Define "Love"

But wait a minute. We need to think about what

the Bible means when we speak of "love."

Americans tend to think of love as an emotion—and we throw it around rather casually. We "love" lasagna and baseball and the latest song.

For many people, love is an emotion, a gooey thing that comes and goes. A man and woman are madly in love with each other, then, the next thing you know, they can't stand one another. If love were an emotion, that wouldn't be surprising.

But the Bible doesn't speak of genuine love as a fleeting, transient feeling. Love is a powerful commitment, a covenant, that begins in the heart of God. It is an insistent force that is selfless. Love is an unbreakable contract: "I am going to bless you, and it doesn't matter whether you deserve it or not, or how I feel that day, or how much I have to sacrifice. I'm giving myself wholeheartedly to acting in your best interest."

That kind of contract goes against almost everything about the way the world acts and thinks. That's why it's so powerful, and that's why we can only find it, in its purest form, in God. We know He loves us perfectly, and He commands us to love Him the same way. No, our love cannot be as perfect, but we make a covenant to accept God's love and to love Him back.

There are times when it's hard to do that. You have a bad day; you ask for something in prayer, and you don't get it. You feel as if God is hiding from you. But remember, this is not an emotion—it's a set policy. You keep on loving God, praising Him, and serving Him, and you'll find that the feelings follow. Actions always set the pace for emotions.

It's a bit like the vow we make when we marry—we will stand by them in sickness and in health, for richer or for poorer, as long as we both shall live. We make the vow before a minister, before God, and before the people we care most about, and the meaning is that this is official. It is permanent. And we're not going to walk out the first time we're in a bad mood.

Another example is the commitment we have to sports teams. Lots of us who love football or basketball or baseball pick a team and follow them for a lifetime, regardless of their championship potential. For instance, some people are devoted to the Chicago Cubs, and it doesn't matter how long "the curse" lasts, how long before the Cubs finally win a pennant.

Many men live and die with their teams. Their love is a policy, a one-sided contract, and the emotions follow.

In the same way, our love for God should be unbreakable, set in stone, engraved in our hearts. Our lives are going to be built around our love for God. Many things could change, but we vow that we will only love God more deeply, no matter what.

So the first thing men must do is to commit themselves heart, mind, and soul to God. If you can do that, you're a long way down the road to being a father by the Book.

Chapter 4

Created to be at Peace

*J*esus spoke clearly about the need to love God. That covers the first four commandments the Pharisees were concerned about. What about the other six?

Jesus says the second greatest commandment is much like the first—but this time it's about loving people. God loves them, and He expects us to do the same. That's hard enough, but there's a built-in challenge with this commandment. And I believe men stumble over it frequently.

Jesus says to love others *as we love ourselves*. There's an assumption here that we *do* love ourselves. It's harder than it sounds. But we can't truly love others if we don't first address the insecurities, frustrations, and anxieties that grow out of our discomfort with who we are. This is crucial because such issues have a way of undermining how we deal with others.

Jesus wants us to have a healthy self-love— not a self-absorption, but a self-acceptance and self-respect—that allows us to let that love overflow into loving others.

It makes us a little antsy to talk about loving ourselves. Men are taught to be doers, active people, rather than reflective, self-examining people. But deep down, if they got in touch with their hearts, they would find that they're very hard on themselves. They're driven. They look at their role models and feel they've fallen short. They haven't built that mansion for their family; they haven't started their own business and become millionaires.

We have to come to a point of being able to say, "God loves me for who I am, and if He can accept me, I must accept myself." Our instruction manual, the Bible, is insistent that we examine our hearts; that we deal with what we find; and that we give it over to God and be at peace.

Have you done that? The heart of the matter is the matter of the heart.

Men need to look deep into their hearts. They need to reflect more, to think about who we are on the inside, where it really matters.

Your Secret Identity

Many men were taught, "Big boys don't cry." No wonder we're so uncomfortable with emotions— anyone's emotions. We can't even identify our own most of the time. So we don't want anyone to let it all hang out; we encourage them to stuff it all back in!

But what are we going to do when the bottom falls out? How are we going to handle life when it all goes wrong, and we don't even have the first clue how to process our emotions, not to mention any male friends who can help us deal with our pain?

Our typical battle plan for that scenario is not a good one. It's to hide behind the mask. You know that tough guy mask that so many men try to wear? Once it was John Wayne, then it was Clint Eastwood. We think we can be that guy who's so tough that feelings just don't apply. But life doesn't work that way.

Ever notice that the superheroes wear uniforms or masks, and most of them are men? They're ordinary guys, meek, mild reporters, but they put on a disguise to go do the heavy lifting. They give us those comic books when we're little boys, and we grow up thinking that's how it works. You can't see tears behind a mask. Batman doesn't go to a therapist. Heroes are supposed to be indestructible.

You could imagine Clark Kent getting discouraged, maybe needing to talk about his feelings. But that's not the kind of guy Lois Lane is enamored with, right? He has to wear a cape and leap tall buildings in a single bound to catch her eye, or so we're led to believe.

Life is not a comic book. It takes a lot less than kryptonite to make us weak. Unfair bosses weaken us. Trouble with our children weakens us. Career frustration weakens us. Lust, deception, fear, greed, and ego constantly seek occasions to weaken us. We're going to have to start dealing with these issues, and forget the cape. Forget the "secret identity." This is the only identity you have; this is *you*. Learn to look into your heart and understand what's there.

God takes us right where we are, as we are, and encourages us forward. He doesn't care about masks or shows of invulnerability. As a matter of fact, He became a man and made Himself completely vulnerable because He loves us so much. That's the true definition of a superhero—not infinite strength, but enough love to set that strength aside if that's what it takes to reach someone.

This is what Christ did for us. It's all in the manual—you can look it up.

Jacob Gets a Grip

Jacob is one more Bible character who is *real*—really flawed; really unlikeable at times; really loved by God all the while. He's another example of the very kind of person God chooses to transform. He's someone just like you or me. God specializes in fulfilling His purpose despite the messes we make—Jacob is proof of that.

Jacob was making trouble literally from day one. Genesis 25 tells us about two twins who were born a few seconds apart. They weren't identical twins; far from it. One was hairy and quite the alpha male from the day he was born. His name was Esau, and he came out first. In ancient culture, that meant everything; it made him the heir to the majority of his father's holdings.

The second son, Jacob, just missed that, and strangely enough, he seemed to realize that close didn't count. When Esau came out of the womb, there was a little hand on his heel, and it was Jacob, wrestling for first place. As a matter of fact, Jacob did a lot of wrestling. He was destined for turmoil, trying to get a grip, as we'll see.

Jacob was the yin to his brother's yang. If Esau was destined to be the man's man, Jacob was the momma's boy. We never read about him out hunting, trapping, getting sweaty. He hung out at home.

They gave him a name that meant "trickster, deceiver," once they saw those little baby fingers wrapped around his brother's heel. The name became a self-fulfilling prophecy. The formative years of his life were notable for the fast ones he pulled on others—and, in a great irony, a fast one someone pulled on him.

You may know the story of how Jacob plotted to get his older brother's birthright. He waited until Esau was very hungry, having been out hunting in the wilderness for days. Jacob cooked up a really nice stew. He had it all bubbling when dog-tired, starving Esau approached.

Esau smelled the food and no doubt his stomach began to growl like the MGM lion. At that moment, he probably would've given his right arm for a bowl of that stuff.

Jacob suggested a simpler swap, and that's how Esau lost his inheritance.

You can imagine how good that food tasted—right up until the bowl was empty. Perhaps Esau took a nice nap, and then realized what he had just done. I imagine he had a bad case of indigestion. The eldest son gets twice the inheritance, so Esau had traded away half of what he could've enjoyed, along with the privileges and responsibilities of overseeing the family name and enterprise upon his father's demise.

There was still the matter of the blessing. It wasn't just about having a verbal contract; you had to have your father, the patriarch of the family, lay hands on you and give you the official blessing. It was an important moment in ancient households.

Jacob was whispering with his mother. He was her favorite, and she helped him pull a lot of his scams. Jacob said, "What am I going to do? If I show up instead of Esau, Dad will have a fit! He's going to know that we're trying to deceive him. What can I do?"

His mother thought about that and said, "You know what? Isaac can't really see too well anymore. If you go in there and talk in a deeper voice, and wear an animal skin, he'll think you have hairy arms and he'll think, "Hey, this feels like Esau.""

You can see where Jacob inherited his shiftiness.

Jacob took the suggestion. He snuck into the meeting playing the role of his brother.

So he had pulled it off.

Or had he?

You Can't Con a Con Man

Soon there was another problem that his schemes hadn't covered. People were saying, "I wouldn't be in your shoes, my friend. You ought to hear how Esau is talking about you. There's smoke coming out of his ears. You'd better watch your back if you know what's good for you."

Jacob wasn't the stand-and-fight type; he was more of the throw-a-sucker-punch-and-run type. So he decided to take off. I think Jacob must have sat by his campfire, listening to creatures howl in the woods. He may have thought about the nasty stuff inside him that brought him to this place. Have you ever felt like that?

The truth is, when we lie and deceive, we hurt ourselves even more than we hurt others. Jacob, shivering out in the wilderness, is a picture of what we do to ourselves—how we isolate ourselves because of the junk inside us that we fail to deal with.

Jacob was on his way to his Uncle Laban's place, where his mother sent him to lay low until things calmed down. In one of the great ironies of the Bible, Jacob ran into someone trickier than himself. Laban had a daughter named Rachel, and she was a knockout. Jacob saw her and began to drool. He went to her dad and put on the charm. Yes sir, no sir. He talked about his plans, his great inheritance, and what a good life he could make for Rachel.

Laban said, "Sounds good, young man. Give me seven years of hard work. That way I'll know you're really committed and I'll give you my daughter."

Jacob signed off on the deal and gave seven tough, backbreaking years of his life. Eighty-four months in the fields. We have to think he did a lot of growing up during that time. And the Bible tells us that the seven years flew by, because he loved Rachel that much.

At the end of this time, he comes to Laban to claim his prize.

That's when he discovered that it takes a con man to know one!

Jacob can't believe it! He gets the older daughter instead of his beloved Rachel.

Laban just smiles and says, "Oh yeah, that's the way it has to be. Now that my older daughter is taken care of, you can marry her sister as well. But that'll cost you another seven years!"

Wrestling Is Real

I believe Jacob must have grown up during the previous seven years, because he doesn't use his newfound buff body to strangle the life out of his father-in-law. Instead, he works seven additional years. He loves Rachel enough to trade fourteen years of hard labor for her.

But the lesson is clear: your sins will find you out. The seeds you once planted are still subject to spring forth in the form of unpleasant consequences. Life just works like that.

The good news is that there can be redemption. When you're chosen of God, failure isn't final!

Jacob eventually reached the point in his spiritual and emotional journey that all of us who would be used by God must come to—the point when we become sick of being controlled by sinful, dysfunctional patterns. We finally see what we're doing to ourselves and others, and we say, "This has to stop—no matter what it takes."

Jacob had gotten into some problems with Laban, his father-in-law. None of Laban's sons liked him very much. So here he was, on the run again, mending fences, dealing with junk. And on top of that that, he was on his way back home to make peace with Esau. It had been twenty years since he left home, and who could know what state of mind Esau was in? Esau might have been fine-tuning his plans of vengeance all this time.

But Jacob had to finally get things right. He was just about at the end of his rope. He'd had enough. So he was trying to sleep, trying to get a grip. In the night, he wrestled. Now you and I do that all the time; we can't sleep because we're wrestling with some problem or decision. But this was *real* wrestling. Nothing about it was rigged. God sent an angel to make sure Jacob got a true workout.

Jacob realized that when someone comes from heaven, that's a good thing. And he said, "I will not let you go unless you bless me" (Genesis 32:26). And at that moment, he finally got a grip. He got such a good wrestling hold on the angel that the match went all night. The Lord blessed him; He changed his name (which, in Bible terms, meant that he changed his destiny). Jacob was now "Israel." The nation that would spring from his family, with all its promise to the world, would take the name of an ex-deceiver.

I think most men know what it means to wrestle through the night, to come to a point of weariness in which we say, "I've had enough. I'm tired of all this." But what comes next? Wrestling a little longer, but wrestling with heaven; proclaiming, "I'm not letting go until God blesses me. I'm not letting go until I have a brand new future. I'm not letting go until I really have a grip on what God wants for me." It's a matter of wrestling until God wins, because when He does, you win also.

Fatherhood by the Book means laying the right foundation. We as men need to love God with all that is within us. And we need to love others, which begins with loving ourselves. Because the fact is, we can't love God or people correctly if what's in us is broken and in disarray.

And sometimes we're going to have to wrestle — with our past; with our personal self-acceptance; and particularly with God Himself. We need to say, "God, I won't let go until you give me a blessing. Give me a new destiny."

Where will you start, men? God is raising up a new army. He wants men after His own heart, and that means you'd better get after *your* own heart. Find out who you are and get in touch with how you feel — knowing, all the while there's no part of you that God won't heal and transform, so that you can be the man He has destined you to be.

A man who isn't at peace with himself will be hard pressed to raise children who are. It's time to be honest — honest with God, honest with yourself, honest with your spouse, and honest with others who are on the road of spiritual authenticity. Like Jacob, get a grip.

In a funny kind of way, wrestling leads to peace.

Chapter 5

Created to be Present

*U*p to now we've talked mainly about the prerequisites. You may be saying, "I thought this was a book about fathers. What you've shared so far easily applies to mothers, cousins, or anybody else!"

That's true. We've carefully dug our foundation, because if you don't get that right, whatever you build on top of it just won't stand. But now it's time to turn our attention to some specific principles that fathers, in particular, should focus on. In each remaining chapter, we'll discuss one of these principles.

The first of them is very simple—simple, yet profoundly important. It is to *be there*.

Being there simply means that you make it a point to show up. It doesn't even require that you do anything particularly outstanding once you're there.

But you'd be surprised how many fathers flunk out right here, at the most basic level of fathering. They fail to show up. This is why the prophet talked about the hearts of fathers turning homeward. Those fathers need to be a literal presence in their children's lives, helping to set things in order.

Something in us is prone to wander. And that thing can make you antsy when you hear the call of the open road, of other activities, of something new or exciting to focus your attention on. Maybe it's the "hunter-gatherer" in you, just as a mother has the "nurturer" profile wired into her mindset. She can hunt pretty well, but she's especially gifted in nurturing. Likewise, man, you can nurture, but being counted on to provide will bring a richer sense of fulfillment.

We need to observe that there are many mothers who, for various reasons, are handling the "gathering" duties. That is, they have to be in the work force outside of the home. And frankly, it suits many of them quite well. The business world is absolutely filled with women who bring excellence and add tremendous value to their professions.

Likewise, there are men who have become excellent at caring for their children and tending to household responsibilities. During the worldwide economic recession of the last several years, we've seen many situations in which men, having lost their jobs, find themselves caring for their children and tending to household responsibilities, at least for the time being.

My only point is to affirm that not all households operate in exactly the same way; nevertheless they can all be blessed. But one thing that won't work is for the father to be perpetually absent. It simply isn't going to fly.

Dad, you were there when that child was conceived, and by God's design you're supposed to be there all along the way. God calls you to being more than a sperm donor. He called you to be a engaged, loving father, a friend and mentor to your children, an encourager and, when necessary, a disciplinarian. You're called to be a model of Biblical manhood and a lifelong inspiration for your sons and daughters. God called you to leave such a mark on your children, and even your grandchildren, that they never forget you or the legacy you leave behind when you've gone from labor to reward.

God calls you to decide in advance that once this life is over, you will have done nothing more important than being present with your children. You recorded the game and watched it later so you could help with homework. You flew home early from that business trip so you wouldn't miss the birthday party. You postponed taking that much needed nap so you could listen attentively and offer counsel and comfort when your child described the pain of being mistreated by schoolmates. Wise choices indeed, because when those moments have long since passed away, their value will appreciate like a sound investment in the hearts of your children.

And all of that is simply about being present. There's great significance in showing up.

Be There in Spirit

Fathers need to be with their spouses and their children physically. But we need to go a little farther.

We also need to recognize that you can be there without being *there*. Have you ever been with someone who was present in the body, but absent in spirit? Someone who seemed a thousand miles away? Husbands, what if I asked your wife this question, what would she say? Would she lament that when it comes to parenting, you're the invisible man, at least when it comes to emotional involvement?

Some dads make things even worse by engaging with their children only as an enforcer. They take pride in being the parent who puts fear into them, who is impatient or angry, who does little listening, but lots of yelling.

Paul instructs fathers, in Ephesians 6:4, not to exasperate their children. What does that mean? Don't drive them to frustration, because it always backfires. You might have the power to win out now, but they're going to remember it, and they're going to break your heart someday if they feel you didn't listen and didn't provide the love they needed.

A father should be someone a child runs to and not from. Jesus called His heavenly Father "Abba," which means "Daddy." He also told His disciples, in the upper room, how close He and His Father were. It was a relationship of pure love and pure dependence. It's also the model for how we should be with our children.

What's the rest of Paul's verse in Ephesians? Don't exasperate them, but, "instead, bring them up in the training and instruction of the Lord." Training and instruction require time. They require your physical and emotional presence and particularly your patience.

I'm not saying it's wrong to get tired. I'm not saying it's going to be easy or convenient. Parenting isn't for the weak or cowardly; it's one of the hardest thing to do in life. But nothing is more important than how you respond to your children. You need to be there spiritually and emotionally.

You might be reading this as a father with older children, who has already made some of these mistakes—who didn't know better at the time. I'm not here to beat up on you. As I said earlier, with God there's always the hope of redemption.

It may be a very difficult situation now. Perhaps your children now live in a different home, because you're divorced and your wife remarried. Perhaps your children are bitter toward you. Every situation is different, but you need to get godly counsel. The most important thing you can do is tell your children you love them, and show them you mean it. Apologize with sincerity for whatever may have happened in the past. It's not too late to be present and involved.

I've seen many incredible things happen when fathers sat down and wrote their child a letter, or took them to dinner, and explained how they made many mistakes, but they want to make amends; how they love their children more than anything in the world; how they simply want to *be there* now, even if they didn't do a great job of it in years gone by.

There may be some bitterness that has to be overcome. But what child does not want to have the love of his or her father? You can overcome those obstacles. The love of God is the most powerful force in the universe. In the end, nothing will hold out against it.

Love is many good things, and the most basic of all is that it's *present*.

What Happens When We're There

It's amazing how research bears out this principle. We know that in homes where the father is present, involved, and loving, the children are far more likely to do better in school. They're less likely to get involved in bad things, and they're more likely to be successful down the road as college students and beyond.

For single moms reading this book, it doesn't mean that your parenting efforts are doomed if there is only one parent under your roof. God is still there, and all things are possible. There are many resources available to single parents who want to do an outstanding job, and the fact is that history is filled with successful people who were raised by a single parent. Please don't be discouraged.

But if we're playing the odds, we know they're stacked in our favor with a loving father and mother in a household. That's simply the way God designed things, and the way it works best. Children with the opportunity to have dad and mom working together to raise them, who are modeling married love, who are modeling the sharing of their skills, will flourish.

Simply put, a father's calling is to put fatherhood before anything else in life other than his relationship to God and to his wife. Of course, these three things don't compete. They work together perfectly, like a stool with three legs holding up a great life. Love God, love your spouse, love your children.

The power of simply being there is such that you can be a fantastic father to a child you didn't bring into this world. It's difficult being a stepfather, but I've seen many of them who are absolutely as beloved by their stepchildren as if they'd been the father all along. The reason is that they're the ones who have been there. They're the ones who have shown love through the sacrifice of time. Love is so powerful that it's often thicker than blood. A father is someone who shows up. A father is someone who cares and who gives.

I've also seen single mothers who dragged a man into the house, thinking that a male was the missing link. But not every male is a man. So involving yourself with just any ol' dude and then forcing your children to be nice to him won't fix the problem; it will only make things worse. And the last thing children need is an endless procession of "uncles" who come and go. What will they think about men after that kind of pattern?

Don't be discouraged if some of these points are a bit painful. Sometimes truth hurts. But like a scalpel, truth only cuts to heal; it's never a knife designed to kill.

There's much more that we need to talk about. But it all starts with being present, with showing up.

Chapter 6

Created to be Priests

*J*ob is an interesting character in the Bible—a compelling one.

He's a man who suffers, who loses everything at one point, and still shows that it's possible to be godly when the bottom falls out. He's also a loving dad.

What interests me is something hardly anyone notices about this book of Job. The Bible tells us, in Job 1:5, that his sons would have these great banquets and invite their sisters. Obviously his extended family got along famously.

Then, after these great banquets had run their course, Job would go before the Lord on behalf of his children. He'd offer burnt offerings for each one, in case one sinned and displeased God in his or her heart during all the revelry.

This is a man who has everything going for him. All his children are speaking to him, they're all inviting each other to parties, and still he worries about what's on the inside; what's in their souls. The Bible tells us he did this regularly.

What I see is a man who took nothing for granted. Many parents are happy as long as everything looks all right with their kids—their hairstyles aren't too wild and they don't wear those saggy pants that need to be hiked up over their behinds. In short, as long as they're good kids who make good grades and relatively good decisions, we're usually content.

But fathers need to be more like Job, thinking, "I don't know every temptation they're facing. I may not be aware of their deepest struggles or how the devil is scheming against them. So I'd better go before the Lord and intercede for them."

Once a father does that, he is a priest in full.

Standing in the Gap

Burnt offerings are no longer necessary because Jesus' death on the cross gave us direct access to the heavenly Father in prayer. But we can and should continue the longstanding practice of praying for others who are in need of divine help. God still wants us to come before Him interceding for one another, just as Christ intercedes for us.

As a matter of fact, nearly everything Jesus did on earth, He did as a model for us to imitate. He cared for the poor so that we would care for the poor. He helped hurting people so that we would help hurting people. He spoke truth to power to show us how to do the same. But most importantly,

He prayed for us in John 17 so that we would learn how to pray on behalf of others.

We should begin praying for our children even before they're born. And after they're born, we do well to dedicate them to the glory of God, and in doing so, dedicate ourselves to their nurture.

Job didn't wait for his children to drift away or to go through a bad spell or to get in some kind of trouble. He regularly lifted them up to God. He had worship services built around the future of his children, and the righteousness of their souls.

I've heard too many fathers say, "I don't do prayer. That's my wife's department." Many good women are the ones standing in the gap between God and their children, and God certainly honors that. But there's nothing in the world like a man who takes spiritual leadership, who grabs his wife's hand and says, "Let's pray." There's nothing like a praying dad.

Do you tell your children that you pray for them? Think of the affirmation it would give them to know that you're going to the Lord on their behalf. They can go to bed at night thinking, "My Dad prays about me every single day."

How much more real is God going to be for that child? How much more prone will they be to develop their own relationship with God?

Job's got it right. Pray for your children on a regular basis. Don't wait until you have to pray. Prayer isn't an afterthought—it's a strategy for life and for leading a family.

A House of Prayer

I also want to encourage you to pray *with* your children.

I'm speaking especially of those children in their younger, formative years. You have an amazing opportunity to have these moments of sitting together in God's presence. They'll never forget it.

A great number of parents, of course, have bedtime prayers. That's a special, casual, and quiet time to talk to God together. But it can become somewhat of a ritual. It's a cozy moment, and it feels like tradition, but be certain you're really praying together. Your child needs to see that when you bow your heads and close your eyes together, "Now I lay me down to sleep" isn't just a way to punctuate the day; you're talking to God.

And as your children get a little older, encourage them to talk more casually to God rather than reciting a formula. It doesn't have to sound as if it were written by a poet. Teach them to be comfortable talking to God in a conversational way.

In my home, Meredith and I decided we would pray for and with our children when they were very young. It didn't have to be at bedtime. We would gather everyone in the family room and have a time of prayer together. Even Jet, our dog, attended prayer meetings at home! I believe our kids felt these were special moments that planted the seed of faith in their hearts.

Just as Isaac put his hands on Jacob and blessed him, I would put my hands on my children's head or shoulder as I prayed for them. We have two kids, so I'd pray for one and then the other.

When we moved to California, Alicia was five and Aaron was three. Just as we speak to children on their level of understanding, we would pray the same way. Basic, simple language, very simply in the first years. We'd pray about their play times, about their friends, about school.

We'd pray on their level, but during those moments, you understand, we were always interceding directly to God in our hearts: *Thanks for hearing our children's prayers, O Lord. Help them. Help them to find the right kinds of friends. Help us to be wise in guiding them . . .*

As the children would come in for this time, we'd let them gather around and get settled. Then they knew I would start off by praying for the whole family. I would thank the Lord for His goodness and blessings, and address whatever else was on our family's mind at the moment. Then I would lay hands on Alicia first, since she was the oldest and was sitting closest. Then would come Aaron.

I remember one particular night when Aaron had come in and gotten settled across the room. As I began to pray over his sister, it dawned on him that he was out of position. My arms couldn't reach all the way across that distance to his head.

I was curious to see what he would do at three years old. Our eyes were closed, but I was peeking just a little bit. As I was wrapping up my prayer for Alicia, I saw him scooting across the room and getting into position—he didn't want to miss out on his blessing!

Don't you think God feels the same way about us as we boldly approach His throne in our times of prayer? It's one thing to be there but distant—as we've described some fathers. You can be there but not there, in prayer but not in prayer. When God sees us drawing near, wanting not just words but the touch of His hand, it gladdens His heart. He's going to reach out and touch our lives when we come to Him that way.

A Spirit of Prayer

We started out this way from the beginning with our family, so our kids didn't know any other way.

They expected to pray together as a family so much that it became part of their mindset. We let them know that whenever there was any kind of issue in their lives, we wanted to know about it so we could lift it up to God. And they have appreciated that. They knew we were always interceding for them—and we still are, even though they're now adults.

School, of course, is a big issue for children. We always told them, "Your job is to apply yourself and do well in your studies."

We didn't let our children decide whether they would be good students or not. We handled them with the expectation that they *would* be good students.

Then, of course, we taught them good study habits. And finally, we said, "If you have an exam coming up, or a big project of some kind, let us know about it so we can pray together."

And sure enough, they would come and tell us. "Big exam on Friday."

"Have you prepared? Are you on top of the studying?"

"Yes."

So they understood faith and works went hand in hand. They had a task—to study well. Then God would bless them.

Then they'd come back with the praise report, and we had something to thank God for. That pattern worked well throughout their scholastic years. In fact, they graduated with honors from both high school and college.

You see what's possible? We can instill in our children a spirit of prayer. By the time they become young adults, your children can have a long record of taking their concerns to God and seeing how He answers their prayers and meets their needs.

At the same time, what's been happening? They've been coming not only to their Father in heaven, but also to their father on earth. They've learned that they can come to you with anything on their minds.

Every home needs an attentive and loving priest. You don't need fancy robes. You don't need an altar or any of the other Old Testament trappings. All you need is a heart of love for your children, a solid faith in God, hands that are ready to love and bless, and a voice to teach your children the words of prayer to their Creator.

Chapter 7

Created to be Prophets

A priest is someone who *speaks to God on behalf of others*. But a prophet is someone who *speaks to others on behalf of God*.

Just as the priest says, "Lord, here are the needs of my children," a prophet says, "Children, here is what God says to you."

As fathers, we need to be speaking for God. We need to be the prophets in our children's lives. It will come from your own understanding of Scripture, and your own personal prayer and time with God. It will also come from your personal experience and wisdom as a believer.

Our children need to see that God is always speaking, always involved with what's happening in the world. He's not way off in heaven, aloof from our issues—He is here and He cares about everything we care about. When your children face questions and problems, God has something to say about those things every single time.

My favorite passage in the Bible about this kind of parenting is just below. We've already dealt with the first part of it—the command to love God with all that is within us. But consider the rest:

> *Hear, O Israel: The LORD our God, the LORD is one. Love the LORD your God with all your heart and with all your soul and with all your strength. These commandments that I give you today are to be on your hearts. Impress them on your children. Talk about them when you sit at home and when you walk along the road, when you lie down and when you get up. Tie them as symbols on your hands and bind them on your foreheads. Write them on the doorframes of your houses and on your gates."* Deuteronomy 6:4–9

As we've seen in earlier chapters, there is a great assumption that the father of the household is setting the pace in honoring God with his life. If you love and serve God, your children see a powerful example. If you don't, then they won't hear your words.

We don't choose whether to teach our children. We teach them—period. We teach them in words, and far more powerfully than that, we teach them through how we live. When children are very small, they pick up on all the little things about their parents.

You're teaching them by telling them they don't

have to go church. You're teaching them by not praying together. Those are lessons, too, and sometimes they're the ones that are most likely to stick. For every principle you teach through instruction, there are many others you teach by omission.

You wouldn't pay it any mind if your children expressed that they didn't feel like going to school on a particular day. Not "feeling like it" wouldn't be enough, right? So why would a parent consider allowing dependent children to stay home from church for no good reason?

If you teach your children, by words and actions, that nothing is more important than God and His involvement in daily life—they will learn that lesson just as they'll learn not to touch a hot stove or play in traffic. Children are amazing learners. It's just a matter of what we decide to teach them.

Therefore we will pray as a family. We will seek His will in all our decisions. We will attend church to learn more about Him, and to participate as parts of the body of Christ. And in all these things, we will experience deep joy, not obligation.

Deuteronomy gives a picture of what our teaching needs to look like.

On Your Way

Having put God's teachings in our heart, says Moses, we let them be revealed in everything we do. "Impress them on your children" (v. 7). When the word "impress" is used, the meaning is like impressing your initials in the sand with your finger. *Engrave* is the general idea of what we're talking about.

In other words, this isn't about simply speaking some words. This is about feeding truth to your children in such a way that it's there forever.

Think about the truths your parents engraved in you. There are certain things you heard or saw done so many times that they're just part of who you are. Your parents didn't even have to think about teaching those things—it was just who they were—their core beliefs, the things they arranged life around.

It was so consistent, so ongoing that now you hear their voices and recall their attitudes in what *you* do.

We're always surprised when it first begins to happen, because we promised ourselves otherwise. But it just goes to show that, like it or not, the traits of the parents become the tendencies of the children. We teach, even when we don't intend to, and children learn, even when they don't realize it. So be proactive about impressing God's Word on them.

Next Moses says, "Speak of them as you sit in your house, as you walk along the road, as you lie down, and as you get up" (v. 7). Do you think he's trying to make a point? We know he's not being too literal about lying down and getting up; the general idea is this: whatever you do, wherever you go. In the midst of the smallest actions of the day, God's truths are being communicated.

If you're a young parent, you're going to be surprised how quickly your kids grow up and move along. I know it's a cliché, but it's a true one. We always think we have plenty of time, but the time of parenting moves right along. Your baby is five, then ten, then twenty—just like that.

Many parents come to a time when they say, "I wish I'd done things differently. I just got busy with life, and I had no idea they'd grow up so fast!"

You've got to have a plan. You have this short season of incredible influence over these young lives. When they're three, six, ten years old—treasure those moments. You'll never regret whatever time you lose working on career stuff, but you'll regret the time you missed with your children.

The Bible tells us not to waste a moment. Talk about God at the dinner table.

Tell about a Bible verse you just read as you drive them to school.

Instead of debating where to eat lunch on the way home after church, use the time to discuss what was taught that day.

After a TV show, compare the issues in that program to what the Bible says. You'll be surprised how many times you can get a great discussion going.

Life is made up of tiny, precious moments that we cast aside as if they're nothing. Claim them now, and exploit them for the future of your children.

Then we are given some creative advice: Tie God's teachings as symbols on your hands, on your forehead; write them on the doorframe. The Israelites literally did these things, and Jesus called the Pharisees on it for doing so without really meaning it.

Don't panic! You don't have to tie anything to your face, or get the Ten Commandments tattooed on your hands. The point is to be creative in using every moment to reinforce truth of God. It should be a living presence in your home, a part of everything you do.

The key is to be natural and loving as you present the things of God. His truth should simply be a normal and constant presence in everything the family does.

Be a prophet of God in your home. Make it your passion to build a family that loves and serves God in all things.

Chapter 8

Created to be Practical

When there was a rash of school shootings several years ago—Littleton, Colorado, Paducah, Kentucky, and a few others—someone did a study to see what linked these boys who were taking guns into their schools and creating so much bloodshed. One of the strongest common denominators was the lack of a father's blessing. All of these boys had father issues.

We know that many fathers are walking out, and leaving Mom to do all of the parenting. She's working as hard and as well as she can, sometimes below the poverty line.

Meanwhile, we also know that often when Dad leaves, children suffer deeply on the inside as well as the outside. They can carry the scars for many years. As young adults, these left-behind kids will be almost twice as likely to require counseling. They'll be far more likely to get into trouble at school and to have problems passing. They'll be nearly twice as likely to drop out.

We're talking about girls as well as boys. The girls are more than two and a half times more likely to have children before marriage.

Homes with no fathers breed criminals more frequently. Nearly two-thirds of rapists grew up in fatherless homes. Such homes also account for nearly three-fourths of all long-term prison inmates.

The stark reality is, you can take nearly any widespread social problem in our country and link it to the lack of fathers in children's homes. If you're a single mother and reading this, I'm not trying to alarm you, and I'm not saying you have no hope. Far from it—all things are possible in Christ. There are many things you can do to give your children a great future.

My plea is to fathers who still have a chance to be heroes to their children, who still have an opportunity to put their kids on the right path.

We need fathers who can be priests and prophets, speaking to God about their children and speaking to their children about God. But we also need fathers to be *practical* in their teaching. There are so many ways that kids should be able to look to Dad for guidance.

Boys and girls often see Dad as the one who is worldly wise, who knows how things are done out there in the real world. So a father has a wonderful opportunity to teach the little things that make a big difference in his children's lives. He needs to prepare them for their future in very practical ways.

Prepare Them for Relationships

One of the most important categories for practical living is relationships. It's not uncommon to see children who lack appropriate manners. For instance, they constantly interrupt adult conversations without excusing themselves, they bump into people without apologizing, words like "please" and "thank you" are non-existent in their vocabularies—the list goes on and on. At least 80 percent of life is dealing with other people, and such children are receiving no training as it relates to social interaction. Dads were created to join moms in teaching children how to be polite.

For younger children, there's a season of getting ready for school. The day will likely come when they come home from school in frustration, because some other child is bullying them. You've got to teach them the finer points of navigating such a situation. You say, "When that kid gives you a problem, here's what I want you to say and do."

Some parents, of course, think the answer is for them, the parents, to personally intervene every single time. So they go to the teacher or to the other parents and make a ruckus. There is a time and a season for doing that, but you make a big mistake if you teach your children that you'll solve all their problems for them. They must internalize the precepts and principles by which they should operate. Dad, that's part of your God-given job description.

Help them learn how to handle each type of problem responsibly, the way Jesus would want them to handle it. Teach them that bad company corrupts good character, and that befriending the right people at school and in the neighborhood is of utmost importance.

As they grow older, of course, there will be different kinds of relationship issues.

How old before you'll allow them to date? Have your answer ready.

How should they behave on a date? Don't leave that unaddressed.

What kinds of parties can they attend? Establish guidelines.

How late can they be out? Curfews are to be your call, not theirs.

Children need boundaries. They need to know where the chalk lines are, what they can do and what is out of bounds. If you let them set all their own boundaries, they'll pay a hefty price, and so will you.

By having clear rules, you can actually take a lot of pressure off your kids. For example, someone invites them to go to a questionable kind of party, and they feel the peer pressure amping up. You've made it possible for them to simply say, "Naw, my dad won't let me go to that kind of party." Such an answer won't earn them cool points with certain peers, but it will assure that they're not around, should some drunken fool or party crasher start a fight or pull a gun!

Puberty can be a storm for both you and your kids; children often have a hard time getting through it. That's a time when their friends are becoming the center of their world, rather than you. It's hard on parents, but it's just life. They still love you, and you need to be patient and understanding, remembering how you were at that age. Be sensitive to your children, attentive even though they may not talk as much to you as they used to. They're not going to be cute seven-year-olds anymore; love them for who they're becoming.

Sometimes your kids will seem like walking jigsaw puzzles; you have to take the little pieces you have, put together all the clues, and figure out what's going on. Watch and listen. Talk to their teachers and befriend their peers parents. Do what you can to help them navigate the confusing world of pre-adulthood.

Teach your daughters what it means to be a young woman of honor, and teach your sons to honor the opposite sex. We all know they have enough poor models of both of those in their world. You be sure and give them the right ones.

And for those of you whose children may even be young adults, you still have work to do. Your children are going to have questions about marriage or parenting, about work, about dealing with bosses, about all the things that come with adulthood.

One of the bittersweet things about parenting is first latching on, then letting go—a delicate dance indeed! You are to give them prime time, attention, and training during those crucial years you have them, while never losing sight of the fact that you're job is to work yourself out of a job! If you teach them the practical things well, they'll be equipped to make it on their own when that time comes.

Prepare Them Financially

Our children need to know how to handle money. When I was growing up, I was given an allowance—not just so I could buy the little things I wanted, but so I could learn to handle money. I had the ability to take that money and blow it on candy, potato chips, soda, etc. But later if I wanted to buy the latest Matchbox car (I had a massive collection of them!), there'd be no money to do it, and the snack items would all be gone. I forfeited something I could enjoy for years to indulge in foods I could only enjoy for hours. Lesson learned.

As parents, we know that we can talk until we're blue in the face, but there are certain lessons our kids will only learn by experience.

We didn't get our allowance because we were cute. We had to earn it through doing our chores, and that was an important lesson, too—the relationship between work and finance, sowing and reaping. If I didn't get my room cleaned and the leaves raked, then there would be no allowance that week.

My parents were careful to make all of it a learning experience. As a very young child, my allowance was a dollar. But I didn't get it in a crisp bill. They gave me three quarters, two dimes, and a nickel. Then they would make the point, "See that dime? That dime belongs to God." They were setting me up to see ten percent of all I received as an expression of worship and gratitude to God.

We were too young to understand all the principles of stewardship, but at least my siblings and I understood from the very beginning that not everything we earned was for us to consume. So as I grew up and eventually got my first job as a paperboy, tithing came easy because it was instilled early.

By the way Dad, you should be a tither too! Don't attempt to teach your children by precept alone—teach them by example as well. In fact, our children can hardly hear what we say for observing what we do. So when it comes to the tithe, show them that it's a joyful seed we sow rather than a legalistic debt we owe. Let them know that while many people rationalize that they can't afford to tithe, the truth is, we can't afford *not* to tithe! If we honor God with the first ten percent of all He gives us, He will bless us in extraordinary ways.

We should also teach our children how to handle the ninety percent well—that after tithing comes saving. Frankly, I didn't learn that lesson properly until much later in life. My dad tithed and gave offerings consistently, so he was able to teach us how to do that. But he had little discipline when it came to saving money. So I was forced to learn the hard way about the importance of saving money and living below my income level. Like most Americans, I spent far too many years saddled with consumer debt. And I learned that while you can get into debt quickly, it takes time, discipline, and sacrifice to get out.

So we would do well to teach our children that delayed gratification is the road to long-term prosperity. You can have what you want, but you can't have it all now!

Prepare Them with Wisdom

New parents quickly discover that they need a lot more wisdom than they have. No one is ever thoroughly prepared to guide a new human being through life. There's a good amount of on the job training.

If you're going to counsel your children through the first crucial years of life, you'll need to be increasing your own wisdom all the time. Leaders must be learners. Whether you lead at church, at work, in the home, or anywhere else, you need to be learning and growing all the time.

Your children will appreciate seeing that you're humble and that you are constantly working to become wiser and smarter. What they won't relate to is a father who wields power rather than leaning on wisdom, and has no desire to grow; a father who uses force and "because I said so" as the be-all end-all of his authority. But when they see you thinking, reflecting, learning more from the Bible and other sources of wisdom, and generally stretching yourself at all times, they will look up to you. They'll know you're doing everything you can to be a good parent.

The book of Proverbs has a great deal to say on this subject, and one of its lessons is, "The beginning of wisdom is this: Get wisdom. Though it cost all you have, get understanding" (4:7). The wording of that may sound strange, but it means that wisdom starts with being wise enough to seek more of it. And even if you find out that the cost is great, keep working to increase your understanding. The saddest sight in life is someone who is happy to be ignorant;

someone who lacks wisdom, and is the only person who doesn't see that he lacks it!

Knowledge, of course, is getting the facts. Wisdom is knowing how to apply those facts. Understanding is the lifestyle of wisdom. The Bible exhorts you to walk in understanding. If you do that, you're a person who knows how the world works, and how to apply the wisdom of God to every life situation. Dad, you want to be wise so you can give your children the chance to be wise.

It means helping your children learn how to think and reason. They'll learn a lot of facts in school, but the wisdom will have to come from the home. Talk with your children about their lives. Help them reason through practical situations. Show them how the Bible's wisdom relates to everything they're going through.

When you walk in understanding, the world can't sell you a bill of goods. We live in a time when so many are out to take advantage of naïve people. Con artists abound. So you need to equip yourself with wisdom to keep yourself out of danger, and you need to help your children do the same.

Chapter 9

Created to be Providers

A basic task of the father is to provide financially and materially for his children.

This directive shouldn't be too difficult for any father to embrace. As men, we tend to enjoy being looked to and counted on. So to meet the responsibility of assuring the financial welfare of our children ought to result in a deep sense of fulfillment. One of the great feelings of satisfaction in life is in knowing we've worked hard and provided the necessities, and even a few comforts, for our families.

Paul, who functioned as a kind of father to Timothy, wrote these words to him: "Anyone who does not provide for their relatives, and especially for their own household, has denied the faith and is worse than an unbeliever" (1 Timothy 5:8).

Worse than an unbeliever? Strong words.

But think about it. What does it say about a believer's faith when he uses his money selfishly, and lets a wife, child, or elderly parent do without? What message does that send to the world? He is worse than an unbeliever because selfishness is diametrically opposed to the very essence of the gospel. We were saved by, and now live to represent, a selfless Savior.

Think also of the effect of this person's actions. He is telling his children, in the most powerful way possible, that he doesn't care about them. He is inspiring bitterness. He is teaching them fiscal irresponsibility. In short, he is being disobedient to God, and he'll be held to account for it.

Perhaps in our world, the place where we most frequently run into this issue is with fathers who have left their homes.

It's unfortunate we have so many broken marriages, but that's just where we are in the real world today. If there has been a divorce or a pregnancy out of wedlock, a dad can still do his proper duty as a provider. The very worst scenario is that of the "deadbeat dad," who has to be pursued and nagged to provide appropriate financial support, especially when he is building his own life, perhaps with a new woman and some stepchildren. He shrugs and says, "I'm not made of money. That's not my problem anymore."

It is his problem, and I'm not even dealing with the legal side of things. Completely apart from the law, a father has the moral responsibility to care for his children, whether he lives under the same roof with them or not.

God doesn't recognize the excuses the father might give; He expects a man to do his duty in full. Our courts may or may not take care of business. But the courts of heaven will. They settle all open cases. Fathers, provide for your children!

When I was growing up, I had friends whose fathers would come in from work after five o'clock in the evening, then sit down and eat; maybe catch a quick nap. Then it would be time to go to the second job. These fathers didn't complain about it; this was what they needed to do to provide for the family.

I believe a man who goes the second mile to take care of his family is worthy of special honor and respect. God is going to bless him for making the decision to be a man of integrity who takes care of business. "For the LORD your God will bless you in all your harvest and in all the work of your hands, and your joy will be complete" (Deuteronomy 16:15).

It may not feel joyful after dragging in from that second job, but I think this father knows what I'm talking about. A man who discharges his duty has a feeling of pride and dignity about him. He is at peace. He respects himself.

By the same token, those who shun their responsibilities become more and more obnoxious. They give their excuses, they look for every loophole, and they talk about their limitations. But when all is said and done, their children are not going to respect them. And until they acknowledge their wrongdoing and repent, they have no basis for respecting themselves.

Helping Your Children Go To College

Some financial experts encourage parents to let their children handle college expenses completely on their own. If that works for your situation, I won't tamper with it. But I must go on the record as saying that in families and cultures where college graduates are not the norm, parents should do more than tell their kids to go to college; they do well to *help* them go.

I speak from experience. I can remember thinking about my dream car, and wondering, *How much longer? When can I get the wheels that I want?*

I wanted to have my fun just like everyone else. But I'd made a commitment to my children. If they excelled in high school and got accepted into the university or college of their choice, I would pay any part of tuition, room and board that wasn't covered by the grants and scholarships they would be awarded.

That kind of promise makes for wide-eyed children. *Wow*, they think—I can go *anywhere if I'll just take care of my end*.

To be sure, giving your children this type of assistance isn't the only way they can benefit from higher education. There are student loans available in most cases. And they can also work their way through college. But to ensure that we created a culture of college graduates in our family, my wife and I agreed to help our kids get undergraduate degrees without starting their adult life with huge debt.

So our children had strong motivation to do their very best in school, knowing that a great gift of education lay at the end of it if they would handle their end. They both did excellently in high school, graduating with honors. And they gave their mother and me a good return on our tuition investment. Our daughter graduated with honors from University of

Southern California and our son graduated with high honors from California State University East Bay.

Provision vs. Entitlement

Children deserve parental support, and they deserve it until they're capable of supporting themselves. That day comes after they've been properly educated and have the resources to work for themselves.

Which brings us to an interesting question about provision. What about parents who have full dependents in their twenties or thirties? How about all these boomerang adults returning to their parents' home with no plan, strategy, or urgency about building a career and becoming independent.

For the last couple of generations, we've tended to pamper our children. Not only have we given them whatever they wanted without training them to work for things; we've also continued to provide everything they need after they've become adults. We now have a situation in which many young adults continue to live with their parents and expect the luxuries they had as children and teens.

Now to be sure, there are some practical reasons why this is happening more now than it did when I was growing up. Unemployment stats are high. Many young adults struggle to get entry-level jobs when there are fewer jobs to be had.

But it also appears that as a generation of parents, we haven't always done the best job of preparing these young people to take care of themselves.

They're accustomed to being cooked for, cleaned for, and cared for while they freelance through life. It appears that in some cases we've created a welfare mentality with our children—an entitlement mindset. Some of our children have it in their brains that someone should always be there to take care of them. So it's our job to give our children a hand up while letting them know they can't keep coming with a hand out.

The problem isn't adult children living at home; it's doing so irresponsibly and with no strategy for appropriate next steps. In fact, I had the privilege of living in my parents' home after college until I married (in my mid-twenties). I was grateful for that opportunity and made sure to not take it for granted.

I believe that if parents allow adult children to live with them, it should be to make the parents' lives easier, their financial load lighter, and/or their quality of life richer. In other words, adult children should be an asset in their parents' home, not a liability.

Parents may well choose to help adult children who are working through a financial hardship. But assisting in a temporary crisis is far different than enabling chronic irresponsibility.

Furthermore, if a parent is facing health challenges, or doesn't want to live alone after being widowed, or has difficulty with some aspect of independence, a live-in adult child could prove very helpful. These too are very different circumstances from the scenario I'm addressing—an indulged kid who won't grow up.

A little girl once saw a new butterfly trying to

fight its way out of a cocoon. She wanted to help, so she reached down and tore open the cocoon and freed the new butterfly. But it couldn't fly. It fell on the ground and had no future but to be eaten by some other insect. Why? Because nature's principle is that the butterfly develop its flying muscles by fighting its way out of that cocoon. It has to do so to survive. God builds these patterns into nature, including human nature. There's a critical time in which those wing muscles have to be built.

If you do your child's fighting for him or her, if you intervene in that all-important process of learning to make a way, you could doom your child to never developing a spirit of competence.

Part of providing, then, is not supplying needs. Ironically, it's restraining ourselves from supplying, once the time has come.

You need to provide for their future by preparing them mentally and emotionally to care for themselves. Let them know what you expect over the long haul, starting when they're teenagers; give them a fair period of time by which they should be making their own way. And be flexible when the situation calls for it.

Pray with them about finding a direction, and give them your blessing. And of course, your home will always be open to them for crisis or for counsel. But "there is a time and a season to every purpose: "a time to plant and a time to uproot"(Ecclesiastes 3. 1-2).

There might be some pushback. Sometimes they will say, "There aren't any *good* jobs available."

You should reply, "Well, then I guess you'll have to get a bad one."

No one has an entitlement to start with an easy and high-paying job. Many generations of the past have started at entry level and paid their dues. They punched the clock, proved themselves capable, and got themselves promoted into better positions. That's a biblical pattern—study the story of Joseph or the book of Daniel. You'll find young men who were in challenging situations and they made the most of them. If your son or daughter wants to wait until a plum job is served on a platter, they'll still be sleeping on your sofa decades from now.

But the bottom line is this: Dads, provide for your children, no matter what sacrifices you have to make. Take care of their needs. Prepare them to be healthy and fruitful adults. It will give you peace and satisfaction like few other things.

Chapter 10

Created to be Protective

*H*ere's another point that fathers should easily embrace: *protecting* their families.

Men like providing and protecting. It's just in their DNA to be the hunter and gatherer who carries out the tough, physical tasks for his family. If someone wants to come at your children, they'll have to go through you.

Numbers 32 tells how the children of Israel were about to cross over the river into the Promised Land, after a generation of wandering and waiting.

Israel was divided into twelve tribal groups. Most were destined to find their inheritance in Canaan. But the Reubenites, the Gadites, and half the tribe of Manasseh spotted land east of the Jordan that they considered ideal for their style of living. The men of these tribes came to Moses and said, "Listen, we have a lot of livestock and these look like perfect acres for grazing. Is it okay by you if we stay back here instead of making the crossing?"

After they assured Moses of their willingness to cross over and fight with their brothers until every tribe had their allotted land, Moses said, "Okay then. Come help us fight. Afterwards, you can cross back over to the east side and rejoin your wives and children."

The spokesmen said, "Fair enough. But first we need enough time to fortify our settlements over here so our families will be protected while we're gone."

And that's exactly what happened. This is just an example of the biblical understanding that our first duty is always to protect the family.

Our homes need to be safe places for our families to live—places where they feel secure and at peace. We need to do everything within our power to get into a safe neighborhood, and once there, to install a good alarm system or get a good watchdog.

Quick story. In my family growing up, we enjoyed several pet dogs over the years. Only one of them was a good, mean watchdog—a black shepherd. You didn't want to get on the bad side of that dog—if he felt that any of us were threatened in any way, he was ready to rock. And that made us feel good.

But when I got married and we started our family, Meredith and I wanted to have a dog that was good with children. We ended up with a black lab. We named him Jet because he was jet black. My hope was that not only would he be cute and friendly with the kids, but that he'd have a little nastiness in there somewhere that would come in handy in a tough spot.

I was disappointed. That dog must've known Jesus as his Savior 'cause he sure loved everybody! I never had the assurance that if push came to shove, he'd take a bite out of an intruder. So we just enjoyed him as a member of the family…and I had an alarm system installed!

Ever Vigilant

There's physical protection, then, but there are other kinds, too.

You want to protect your children from bad influences. How can you do that? It's a lot harder than installing an alarm system or getting a mean dog. When your kids are little, you can oversee every part of their lives. But as they get older, there are more hours in the day when they're somewhere outside your reach—particularly if you're a working dad. They're going to want to find their friends, and you have to do what you can to teach them how to find the right ones.

I taught my two that I wanted to know who they were hanging with, and I wanted to know they'd choose the right kind of friends. When they were young, we started teaching them about that. Now this didn't mean being snobbish. We taught our kids to be kind and good to everyone the way Jesus would, and never to look down on anyone. But that doesn't mean they have to be best friends with everyone.

You may get static from your teenagers when you want to know where they're going, and who they'll be with. But you can't back down. Who are the families of their friends? What are the rules in that household? As I mentioned earlier, these are thing you need to know.

Make rules to protect your children, and let them know exactly what those rules are. Again, you might get some whining and grousing, but stick to your guns.

Protect your children not only in body but in spirit. Unhealthy images and messages are all around us today, aren't they? Turn on the television, and you're not going to find only family-friendly stuff like in the days when I grew up. Back then, when there was only network television, you could count on wholesome programming. Suffice it to say, you can't count on that anymore. We have a thousand channels and most of them filled with things you wouldn't have imagined seeing on your home TV decades ago.

You need to decide early on what your kids can and can't see. I'm not here to tell you to throw the television out the window. But if you have a modern set, there are ways to parent-protect the worst channels. And of course, you want to set a good example. Don't have them walking through the room and you lunging for the remote to switch the channel. You're their model. Think hard about the life they see you leading, the values they see you embracing. Part of your protection is the example you set.

The Internet is another threat that we could never have anticipated before the days of personal computers. So many things unhealthy for children are a few clicks away. Fathers, don't let your children use the computer without guidance. Where appropriate, take advantage of the filters and stopgaps to block certain kinds of content from your computers. Do your homework. Find out what you'll need to do to protect the minds and spirits of your children and yourself.

Ultimately, the best protection you can offer will be the training of their minds. Teach them to think biblically. Help them understand why some things are good and spiritually healthy, and other things aren't. Watch TV together when feasible—don't break up into rooms where everyone has a separate show. Watching things together can provide insight into whether or not your children are learning to discern right from wrong.

There's never a way to fully and completely protect your children. They have to live in a world that's filled with darkness. As they grow older, you begin to lose that total control you had when they were babies. They begin to make their own choices. But by that time, if you've loved them well, taught them well, and prayed with them well, chances are they're going to make you proud. And even if they take some ill-advised detours and depart from the truth you've imparted, that truth will not depart from them. Like the prodigal son in Luke 15, who is the focus of the next chapter, they'll be able to find their way home.

You may be praying for your children harder and more frequently than you ever have before. But be assured that God will honor the investment you've made in covering their lives with love and protection.

Chapter 11

Created to be Passionate

*T*he greatest story Jesus ever told was the one about the young man known as the Prodigal Son. It's found in Luke 15.

He asked for his inheritance early so that he could go and throw it away, waste it on wild parties, women, and wine. He made the decision that is every parent's nightmare—the decision to rebel against everything he was ever taught.

We've talked about protecting your children. There comes a time when you feel helpless, because your children have the ability to simply walk away. You worry that the next disagreement will push them away from you. Once they get a car and a little income, the balance of power shifts in that they can simply leave.

You have to pray that all the teaching you've done, all the love you've given, will make a difference. But sometimes there are other influences that get in, no matter how hard we try to keep them out.

Sometimes our kids simply want to sow a few wild oats, and all we can do is pray and be there for them.

But whenever I read this story in Luke, I'm struck by the passion of the father, who was out waiting for his son to come home. The boy had been gone long enough to go through his inheritance. He was probably wasted away to almost nothing, because Jesus tells us he was starving. He was now taking care of someone's pigs which, to the Jewish mind, was the lowest form of labor imaginable. And he was tempted to sneak and eat the stuff he fed to the pigs.

This young man had broken his father's heart, dragged his name through the mud in public, and thrown away one third of the money the father had given his life to save. You can imagine how a lot of fathers would handle that situation: "I have no son!" They would lock their doors and turn away, and few people would blame them.

How did the son know he could come home? I'm sure it's because he knew the character and compassion of his father. He knew that his dad would never stop loving him, despite having suffered incredible disappointment. As modern day parents, we have the years of their childhood to make our children see that: "Son, daughter, no matter what you do, I will always love you. I may be disappointed with you or disapproving of some of your choices, but nothing could ever get in the way of my love for you."

Children need to know that for certain.

I think the Prodigal Son knew he could always go home. Clearly, he didn't have any internal assurance that he would be received again *as a son*, but he knew that his penitence wouldn't be ignored. So he rehearsed a little speech as he walked home. His hope was that he would be allowed to join the ranks of the servants in his father's house.

Boy, was he in for a surprise! When the father spotted his son walking back home, he ran (not walked) down the road to meet him. He threw his arms around the boy, and the boy started in on his rehearsed speech of contrition. But clearly the father wasn't listening. He was too busy shouting commands to the servants: "Kill the fattened calf! Clean up the house! Invite our neighbors and friends! Hire a good band! We're going to have a big party! And quickly bring a robe and sandals and a ring! *My son* is alive and back home!"

That father's love for his son was a bottomless well that could never run dry. It was powerful. This once disgustingly disobedient son who genuinely repented discovered just how amazing grace can be.

Jesus told this story, of course, to make a point about the depth of God's love for you and me. There's nothing in the world we can do to make God stop loving us. Each one of us has deeply offended our heavenly Father at so many times and in so many ways. Yet He loved us and anticipated the day when we would come to ourselves.

Don't get it twisted—He never smiles on sin and disobedience. There are ways He cannot bless us until we have come to ourselves and repented. In fact, the only way He can display love toward the rebellious child is to discipline him or her. I don't know about you, but I've experienced the severe discipline of the Lord—it's no fun, to say the least. But even His discipline is redemptive in nature. It's not meant to destroy us; it's meant to destroy the lie that sin is a viable alternative to the will of God.

But again, the striking thing about this story is the passion of the father. That's what we must imitate as earthly fathers.

Leave No Doubt

Have you let your children know how much you love them lately? Have you engraved it in their hearts that there is no way they could prevent your love, no matter how hard they tried? You love them, but do they know it? Have you made it sufficiently clear?

Some of you would admit to having been raised in a home in which your father never told you he loved you. Maybe he couldn't bring himself to say the words. Maybe it never crossed his mind to express love verbally. Or maybe he didn't like what he considered "touchy-feely stuff." For whatever reason, you never benefited from hearing those words from him.

The traits of the parents become the tendencies of the children. But silent, undemonstrated love is a trait you simply can't afford to tolerate in yourself or pass on to the next generation.

We have to let them know by our words, by our hugs, by our time, by our generosity, by our discipline, and for us married folks, by loving and honoring our wives. Even if you're not married to the mother of your children, it says a lot to your children when you are respectful of their mom.

If you had one of those non-expressive fathers, you have to break the cycle. Maybe it will feel funny. Maybe it will seem awkward in the early going. But just do it. We can't afford to leave a doubt in their minds of our love for them.

Think about God. He wanted to be sure we got the message that He loved us. He put on flesh to let us know. He went to the cross to let us know. He took on all the punishment we had earned, to let us know. And he blesses us every day—to let us know.

I once heard a story that stuck with me. It's about a village in Mexico in which a father and his son had a bitter argument. There were terrible words between them, and the son left home in a rage. "This is good-bye forever," he said.

"Fine by me," snapped the father. And the son was gone.

A few months, a few years, and the father's grief only became deeper. There was no word whether his son was living or dead. The old man no longer cared about his pride. He couldn't even remember what the argument was about. All he knew was that he wanted his son back, at any price. Love was greater than disagreement. It survived insults and shouting. When all that dust cleared, there was still love.

So he closed down his home and went looking for the young man. He moved from village to village, with no clue to guide him, until finally he had some pretty good information that his son was alive and living in a certain city.

The father went to that city and placed a small ad

in its newspaper. He wanted to be fairly discreet, so he only used his son's first name. He wrote:

> *Pedro,*
>> *We should never have quarreled. I am sorry, and I miss you. I don't want us to be apart anymore. Please come to the hill on the northwest side of the city at six o'clock p.m. tomorrow. I long to see you.*
>
> *Love,*
> *Your Father*

At the appointed hour, the old father cleaned up, put on his best clothing, and made his way to the top of the mountain with a full, hopeful heart. He was astounded by what he saw. There were hundreds of young men, all of them named Pedro, all with expectant faces, all hoping to be reconciled to their own fathers.

This is where we are, my friends. The world is filled with families that haven't gotten it right; children that have fled in frustration and anger. There are sad faces of fathers and sons and daughters who need each other, all of them waiting for the day when they can be reconciled.

Our God loves us passionately, and we need to respond to His love by loving our children just as passionately. "We love because he first loved us" (1 John 4:19).

After all, the years go by far too quickly. Someday you'll remember what your son was like before his voice got deep, back when he would still sit in your lap.

You'll remember how your daughter thought her daddy hung the moon, that he had all the wisdom in the universe on every subject. That time goes by far too quickly. You've got this time and this season under heaven, and the clock is ticking.

Make the most of it. It won't come again. Love the Lord your God. Love your neighbor as you love yourself. And love your children with a renewed love—passionate, patient, and enduring. It will become their compass for successful lives long after you are gone.

CPSIA information can be obtained at www.ICGtesting.com
Printed in the USA
BVOW040440020512

289142BV00001B/1/P